Fact Finders®

DISGUSTING JOBS
in COLONIAL AMERICA

THE DOWN AND DIRTY DETAILS

BY ANITA YASUDA

Content Consultant:
Kirsten Fischer, Professor, Department of History,
University of Minnesota

CAPSTONE PRESS
a capstone imprint

Fact Finders Books are published by Capstone Press,
1710 Roe Crest Drive, North Mankato, Minnesota 56003
www.mycapstone.com

Library of Congress Cataloging-in-Publication Data
Names: Yasuda, Anita, author.
Title: Disgusting jobs in colonial America : the down and dirty details / by Anita Yasuda.
Description: North Mankato, Minnesota : Capstone Press, 2018. | Series: Fact finders. Disgusting jobs in history
| Includes bibliographical references and index. | Audience: Age 8-10. | Audience: Grade 4 to 6.
Identifiers: LCCN 2017038582 (print) | LCCN 2017039105 (ebook) | ISBN 9781543503739 (eBook PDF) | ISBN
9781543503692 (hardcover)
Subjects: LCSH: United States—History—Colonial period, ca. 1600-1775—Juvenile literature. | United States—
Social life and customs—To 1775—Juvenile literature. | United States--Social life and customs—Colonial
period, ca. 1600-1775—Juvenile literature.
Classification: LCC E188 (ebook) | LCC E188 .Y37 2018 (print) | DDC 973.2—dc23
LC record available at https://lccn.loc.gov/2017038582

Editorial Credits
Editor: Alyssa Krekelberg
Designer: Maggie Villaume
Production specialist: Laura Manthe

Photo Credits
Alamy: Niday Picture Library, 16–17; Getty Images: Ann Ronan Pictures/Print Collector/Hulton Archive, 23, Jack
Milton/Portland Press Herald, 22; iStockphoto: duncan1890, 4, 24–25, 27, FalconScallagrim, 13, Grafissimo, 5
(background), ilbusca, 15, kreicher, 29, Nikola Nastasic, cover (bottom left), ZU_09, 6–7; North Wind Picture
Archives, 28; Shutterstock Images: Africa Studio, 19, Alexandru Nika, cover (bottom right), 26, bonga1965,
14 (right), Gerald A. DeBoer, 14 (left), Ian Dikhtiar, cover (background), Per-Boge, cover (top left), Rainer
Lesniewski, 5 (map), Sergei Primakov, 21, Sergey Lukyanov, 20, Stacey Newman, 9, Steve Collender, cover
(blood), xpixel, cover (dirt); SuperStock: ClassicStock.com, 10–11, Julian Birbrajer/Mauritius, 12

Design Elements: iStockphoto, Shutterstock Images, and Red Line Editorial

Printed and bound in Canada.
010800S18

TABLE OF CONTENTS

A NEW BEGINNING:
FROM 1607 TO 1776

More than 400 years ago, **colonists** crossed the Atlantic Ocean to start new lives in North America. There they encountered many American Indian groups, such as the Wampanoag and Cherokee. These Native Americans had their own distinctive cultures and languages. But this did not stop colonists from taking Indian lands. This time is called the Colonial Period (1607–1776).

Some colonists worked at jobs that were dangerous and disgusting. They worked as tanners, whalers, and hatters. Others were in the colonies involuntarily, and had it much worse. They were the men, women, and children who were sold as enslaved people at auctions.

MAY 14, 1607

Tanners, bricklayers, and doctors are some of the first English settlers at the Jamestown settlement in Virginia.

DECEMBER 1620

Colonists aboard the *Mayflower* establish the Plymouth Colony. They work as farmers and fishers in what is now Cape Cod, Massachusetts.

1630

The Puritans establish the Massachusetts Bay Colony. They work as skilled craftspeople such as tanners, barrel makers, cobblers, and weavers.

1664

New York, New Jersey, and Delaware become British colonies. By 1732, there will be 13 colonies along the Atlantic Coast. Many people work as fur trappers and in the fur trade.

1729

An **apothecary** in Philadelphia becomes the first to make and sell medicines.

colonist — person who settles a new area or country

apothecary — person who makes and sells medicines

BRITISH COLONIES IN 1776

NEW HAMPSHIRE COLONY

MASSACHUSETTS BAY COLONY

PLYMOUTH COLONY

RHODE ISLAND COLONY

NEW YORK COLONY

CONNECTICUT COLONY

PENNSYLVANIA COLONY

NEW JERSEY COLONY

DELAWARE COLONY

MARYLAND COLONY

VIRGINIA COLONY

JAMESTOWN, VA

NORTH CAROLINA COLONY

SOUTH CAROLINA COLONY

GEORGIA COLONY

Enslaved people were whipped as they worked.

CHAPTER ONE

TERRIBLE TANNERS

Tanners turned skins of sheep, deer, and pigs into leather. They even used dog hides. Tanners dug pits into the ground. They soaked the animal skins in there. Men dragged the wet skins in and out of pits filled with urine and **lime**. The lime made the fat and hair melt off. But strings of dangling flesh might be left behind. Tanners used dull knives.

lime — a white substance that comes from bone or shells; used to burn hair off skins

FOUL FACT

Colonists could not always find firewood to use for cooking or staying warm. Instead, they used dried horse and cow dung.

They scraped off the rotting flesh. Tanners also used warm dog poop to help soften the skins. Tanning could require up to 200 steps before a skin was ready to be sold.

After months of work, the skin was ready to be dried. The dried skins were sold to craftspeople. They would turn the skins into shoes and saddles. Some clothing, including jackets, was also made of leather.

DEAR DIARY

Samuel Lane was a tanner in the 1700s when his youngest son, Jabez, began working with him. Jabez learned all about the exhausting, smelly work. To tan the animal skins, he would "put ten hides in a **vat** to soak off the dirt and flesh. . . . More than two weeks later, he 'work'd' the hides, scraping off the debris, and 'put them into the Limes,' where they remained for six weeks."

vat — a large pot or tub used in industry

Animal skins were stretched during the tanning process.

CHAPTER TWO

STINKY SCAVENGERS

Piles of animal bones and poop could be found on colonial streets. In some places the streets were ankle-deep in mud and filth. Colonists emptied chamber pots filled with urine and poop outdoors. They tossed garbage onto the streets. The rotten food attracted pigs and raccoons. More people moved to the colonies.

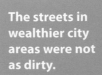

The streets in wealthier city areas were not as dirty.

Garbage problems worsened. In large towns, **scavengers** were hired to clean up.

Their jobs took them down foul-smelling streets. Scavengers cleaned the streets of rotting animals. They went door to door. They took away the overflowing piles of bones and poop outside people's homes. Scavengers piled them onto their small, two-wheeled carts. But the narrow streets still filled up with waste.

chamber pot

scavenger — person who took away garbage in a cart pulled by a horse

Rats feasted on rotten food.

CHAPTER THREE

FORCED, FOUL WORK

Clothing was dyed blue using the indigo plant. Colonists forced enslaved people to do this hard work. Men, women, and children worked under the sun. Their backs ached. They had to stoop over for hours to plant the seeds. They pulled hungry grasshoppers and caterpillars off the plants. Slaves did not have much time off. They worked almost every day from sunrise until sunset.

When the indigo crop was ready, slaves cut the stems. They put the stems and leaves into large wooden pots. The pots were filled with animal urine, lime, and hot water. The slaves let the indigo soak. The smell from the pots attracted swarms of flying bugs.

indigo plant

After slaves collected indigo, they turned it into paste. This paste was used to dye clothes.

Some of these insects spread diseases, such as **malaria**. Most slaves died at a younger age than white colonists. Slaves often died before the age of 30 because of poor diet and hard labor, which increased their chances of getting sick. On average, white colonists lived until they were 50.

Slaves were forced to pick cotton for the slaveholders.

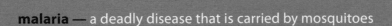

malaria — a deadly disease that is carried by mosquitoes

CHAPTER FOUR

DANGEROUS DOCTORS

In the 1600s there were few doctors in North America. When colonists got sick, some went to see a barber. Barbers didn't just cut hair. When someone had a sore tooth, he or she went to the barber. The barber would give the tooth a good yank to get it out.

Patients with infected fingers and toes also visited the barber. Some of these people had signs of **gangrene**. One symptom was large, black blisters. Smelly pus and blood flowed from these wounds. Barbers cut off the area with a small saw. Its sharp blade ripped through the muscle and bone.

gangrene — an injury that leads to a loss of blood supply to an area of the body, such as the foot

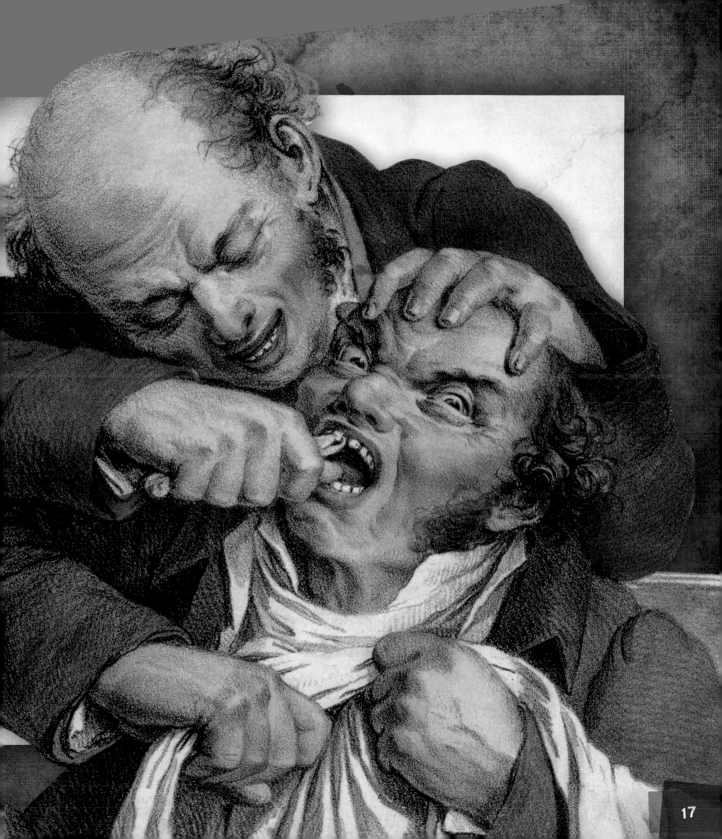

DEAR DIARY

Dr. Alexander Hamilton [no relation to the Treasury secretary] was shocked when he traveled to America from Scotland. He found that many of the people who were practicing medicine didn't know anything about healing people. He thought these "doctors" were no better than butchers. Hamilton believed they had "no knowledge or learning but what they have acquired by bare experience."

Barbers also drew a person's blood. They thought it would heal people. Barber's cut a vein in the patient's arm. Blood squirted into a pan. Sometimes the barbers took too much of the patient's blood. Some people died from the treatment.

Most people in colonial America went to an apothecary when they were ill. Apothecaries also treated the sick. They set broken bones. They also mixed their own medicines. Some medicines included vinegar, breadcrumbs, and earthworms. This mixture was said to cure broken bones. People eventually realized this medicine did not work.

Apothecaries prescribed medicine for patients.

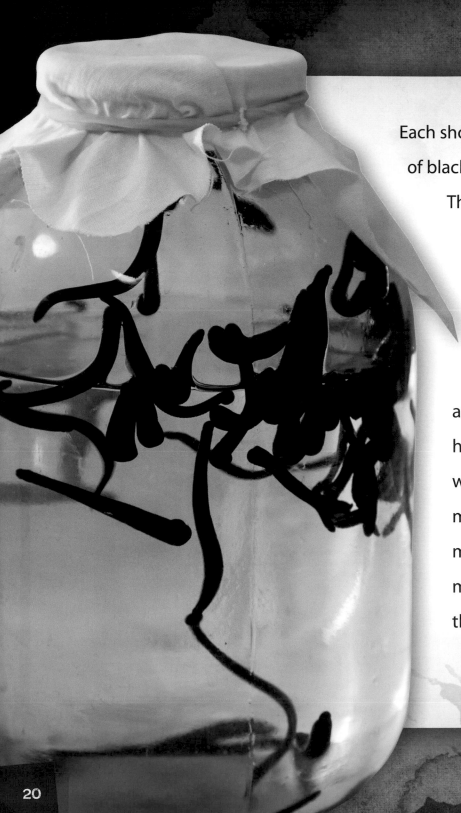

Each shop also had a big jar of black, squirmy leeches. They were used to treat vomiting, belly pains, and hair loss. Some people used leeches to cure headaches and backaches. The hurt area might be washed with warm milk, sugar, and raw meat. Then the leech's mouth was placed on the same spot.

Leeches could be left sucking the patient's blood for up to 30 minutes! Doctors sometimes use leeches today. In surgeries, leech bites help the blood to clot.

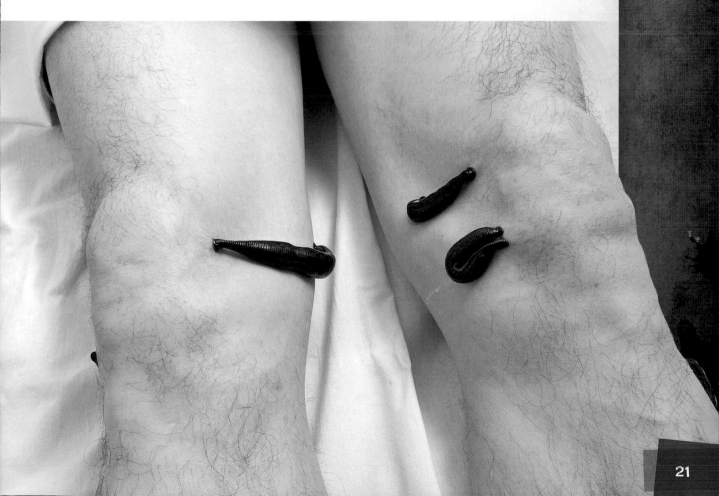

CHAPTER FIVE

HORRIBLE HATTERS

A hatter's job was dangerous and deadly. Many colonial men and women wore hats. Some traders sold hats made from beaver pelts. To make beaver hats, hatters used a chemical called **mercury**. They spread it on the soft undercoat of the fur. Hatters didn't know that the chemical could kill them. They breathed in the mercury fumes. Over time these fumes damaged their **nervous systems**.

beaver fur top hat

mercury — a natural element that is poisonous in the body and can cause health problems

nervous system — cells and nerves in the body that send and receive messages from the brain

23

FOUL FACT

Colonists had lice in their beds, clothing, hats, and wigs. These bugs bit them day and night. The colonists used fine-toothed combs to get rid of the lice and their eggs.

Mercury built up in hatters' bodies. The first sign of mercury poisoning was shaking. The shaking began in their fingertips. Then it spread to their arms and legs. In time their health got worse. Sometimes hatters could hardly walk, speak, or think.

Other colonists believed that a sick hatter was losing his or her mind, or going mad. This might be the origin of the expression "mad as a hatter." Many hatters died young.

The hatter in *Alice in Wonderland* showed signs of madness.

In this Style 10/6

CHAPTER SIX

WEATHERED WHALERS

Whalers did not have much protection from harsh weather, storms, or rough seas. Once a whale was spotted at sea, the crew chased after it. Sometimes they had to race after the whale for many hours. When the whale was close enough, one man threw a **harpoon**. As the whale struggled, men could be washed overboard. The ship could also be dragged under the sea.

From the 1720s on, colonists used larger ships to hunt whales in the deep sea. Whalers spent months away from home. Ships were uncomfortable and cold. The men's blankets and clothes were filled with bedbugs and fleas.

harpoon — a lance with a rope attached to it
blubber — a layer of fat in sea mammals such as whales
baleen — a strong and springy bone-like material in a whale

If they were close to land, whalers towed the dead animal to shore. The men stripped the whale of its **blubber** and **baleen**. They boiled the blubber. Whale guts and clumps of thick flesh were left to rot in the sea.

As the blubber boiled, oil melted out of it. Whalers scooped out the meat and skin as they rose to the surface. They threw it onto the fire to keep it going. Whalers boiled the blubber for days.

If a whale was killed in the deep sea, the whalers would haul the body toward the ship, where they would cut it up.

FOUL FACT

Whalers took a rare, gray wax called *ambergris* from the guts of a whale. At first it smelled like poop. After a while the smell changed, and then the wax was used to make perfumes. A lump of the gray wax could be as large as a baseball. Ambergris was worth so much money that it was nicknamed "Neptune's Treasure," after the Roman god of the sea.

Sailors watched the whale blubber as it boiled.

After the oil cooled, it was put in wooden barrels and shipped. One whale might provide 40 or more barrels of oil.

Colonists used the whale's fat in soaps and candles. Craftspeople used baleen to make fishing poles, canes, and tools. Whale bone was also used to make hoops for hooped skirts and corsets.

THE CHANGING COLONIES

In the 17th century the colonies needed workers. More people left Europe for the New World. Merchants opened businesses. As the colonies grew, so did their dirty problems.

Towns could not stop people from polluting. More people meant more trash piles. Animal guts and dung spilled onto streets. Waste flowed out of homes. No one wanted to wade through this filthy mess.

By 1775 the first shots of the Revolutionary War (1775–1783) were fired. A new chapter in American history was beginning. But there were still plenty of gross jobs. There were rats to catch, teeth to pull, and poop to cart away.

The Founding Fathers signed the Declaration of Independence in 1776. In it, they declared independence from Britain.

GLOSSARY

apothecary (uh-PAWTH-uh-kair-ee) — person who makes and sells medicines

baleen (buh-LEEN) — a strong and springy bone-like material in a whale

blubber (BLUH-ber) — a layer of fat in sea mammals such as whales

colonist (KAH-luh-nist) — person who settles a new area or country

gangrene (GANG-green) — an injury that leads to a loss of blood supply to an area of the body, such as the foot

harpoon (hahr-POON) — a lance with a rope attached to it

lime (LYM) — a white substance that comes from bone or shells used to burn hair off skins

malaria (muh-LAIR-ee-uh) — a deadly disease that is carried by mosquitoes

mercury (MERK-yer-ee) — a natural element that is poisonous in the body and can cause health problems

nervous system (NERV-uhs SIST-uhm) — cells and nerves in the body that send and receive messages from the brain

scavenger (SKAV-in-jer) — person who took away garbage in a cart pulled by a horse

vat (VATT) — a large pot or tub used in industry

READ MORE

Burgan, Michael. *The Split History of the American Revolution.* North Mankato, Minn.: Compass Point Books, 2013.

Morley, Jacqueline. *You Wouldn't Want to Be an American Colonist!* New York: Franklin Watts, 2013.

Vonne, Mira. *Gross Facts about the American Colonies.* North Mankato, Minn.: Capstone Press, 2017.

INTERNET SITES

Use FactHound to find Internet sites related to this book.

Visit www.facthound.com

Type in this code: 9781543503692

CRITICAL THINKING QUESTIONS

1. If you could go back in time, which of the disgusting jobs described in this book would you try? Explain your reason.

2. There were many disgusting jobs in Colonial America. Why do you think people agreed to work at these jobs?

3. In what ways were colonial barbers similar to present-day surgeons? In what ways are they different?

INDEX

ABOUT THE AUTHOR

Anita Yasuda is the author of many books for young readers. Her children's book *Explore Simple Machines!* won the 2012 Society of School Librarians International Honor Book Award for science books, grades K–6. Anita is a history buff who reads and visits historical sites across North America. Anita lives with her family in California.